This Journal Belongs To:

Made in the USA
Monee, IL
19 October 2021

80401858R00056